The Story of
ALL-STAR ATHLETE
JIM THORPE

The Story of
ALL-STAR ATHLETE
JIM THORPE

by **Joseph Bruchac**
with illustrations by **S. D. Nelson**

Lee & Low Books Inc.
New York

Text copyright © 2004, 2016, 2019 by Joseph Bruchac • Illustrations copyright © 2004 by
S. D. Nelson • Photo credits: p. 10: Saukenuk map by NeuStudio, based on material from
Lloyd H. Efflandt's *Lincoln and the Black Hawk War*, courtesy Rock Island Public Library,
Rock Island, Ill. Map copyright © 2019 by Lee & Low Books • p. 12: Library of Congress,
Prints and Photographs Division, LC-DIG-pga-07519. Lithograph by John T. Bowen •
p. 14: Library of Congress Prints and Photographs Division. LC-DIG-ppmsca-05082.
Photograph by A. Zeno Shindler • p. 22: Library of Congress, Prints and Photographs
Division, LC-DIG-pga-11432. Painting by J. O. Lewis • p. 24: The Miriam and Ira D.
Wallach Division of Art, Prints and Photographs: Picture Collection, The New York
Public Library. "Battle Of Bad Axe." The New York Public Library Digital Collections.
http://digitalcollections.nypl.org/items/510d47e0-f799-a3d9-e040-e00a18064a99 • p.
33: Library of Congress Prints and Photographs Division, LC-DIG-ds-03672 • p. 35:
XOS Technologies, Inc. • p. 43: "Richard Henry Pratt" by John N. Choate. Courtesy of the
Dickinson College Archives & Special Collections. All Dickinson College photos that follow
are used under a CC BY-NC-SA 4.0 license, https://creativecommons.org/licenses/by-nc-
sa/4.0/legalcode • p. 46: "Wounded Yellow Robe, Timber Yellow Robe, and Henry Standing
Bear, 1883, #1 [before]" by John N. Choate. Courtesy of the Dickinson College Archives
& Special Collections. • p. 47: "Wounded Yellow Robe, Timber Yellow Robe, and Henry
Standing Bear, 1886, [after]" by John N. Choate. Courtesy of the Dickinson College Archives
& Special Collections. • p. 49: "Yale vs. Carlisle Indians, Manhattan Field, October 24,
1896." First published in *Harper's Weekly*, vol. 40, no. 2081 (October 1896). Courtesy of the
Dickinson College Archives & Special Collections. • p. 50–51: "Panoramic View of Indian
School and Campus, Carlisle, Pa." Courtesy of the Dickinson College Archives & Special
Collections. • p. 58: "Glenn Warner" by Bain News Service. Library of Congress Prints and
Photographs Division. Bain News Service photograph collection. LC-DIG-ggbain-31529 •
p. 74: Public domain. Photograph via Agence Rol

LEE & LOW BOOKS Inc., 95 Madison Avenue, New York, NY 10016 • leeandlow.com
Edited by Philip Lee and Cheryl Klein • Book design by Charice Silverman and NeuStudio
Book production by The Kids at Our House • The text is set in Vollkorn. The display font is
Avenir. The illustrations are rendered in acrylic. • First Edition • 10 9 8 7 6 5 4 3 2 1

Library of Congress Cataloging-in-Publication Data
Names: Bruchac, Joseph, 1942- author. | Nelson, S. D. , illustrator. • Title: The story of
all-star athlete Jim Thorpe / by Joseph Bruchac, with illustrations by S.D. Nelson. •
Description: First Edition. | New York : Lee & Low Books Inc. , [2019] | • Series: The story
of --; 8 | Audience: Ages: 8-12. | Audience: Grades: 4 to 6. | Includes webography. | Includes
bibliographical references. • Identifiers: LCCN 2019020608 | ISBN 9781643790107
(Paperback : alk. paper) • Subjects: LCSH: Thorpe, Jim, 1887-1953--Juvenile literature. |
Athletes--United States--Biography--Juvenile literature. | Indian athletes--United States
--Biography--Juvenile literature. | Football players--United States--Biography--Juvenile
literature. | Football coaches--United States--Biography--Juvenile literature. | United
States Indian School (Carlisle, Pa.)--Football--History--Juvenile literature. | United States
Military Academy--Football--History--Juvenile literature. | Sauk Indians--Biography-
-Juvenile literature. | Fox Indians--Biography--Juvenile literature.Classification: LCC
GV697.T5 B775 2019 | DDC 796.092 [B] --dc23 • LC record available at https://lccn.loc.
gov/2019020608

4

TABLE OF CONTENTS

CHAPTER ONE
BRIGHT PATH

They say Jim Thorpe's story began in May of 1887 in a small log cabin on the North Canadian River. There in the Indian Territory that became the state of Oklahoma, Charlotte Vieux Thorpe, a Potawatomi woman, gave birth to twin boys. Her husband, Hiram, a mixed-blood Indian of the Sac and Fox nation, stood close by on that spring day.

The sun was in Hiram Thorpe's heart as he looked down at the sons he named Charles and James. Jim's mother gave him another name.

"Wa-tho-huck," she said, thinking of how the light shone on the road to their cabin. "Light after the Lightning, or Bright Path."

As good as that name was, neither of them knew just how far that path would lead their son.

Like most twins, Jim and Charlie were close, even though they were not exactly the same. Charlie had darker skin and brown hair, while Jim's skin was light and his hair dark black. When they raced or wrestled, Jim was always a little ahead of Charlie, his best friend. Whenever Jim got too far ahead, he would stop and wait.

"Come on, Charlie," he would say with a grin.

Then, when his brother caught up, they would be off again.

Summer or winter, Jim and Charlie's favorite place was outdoors. They roamed the **prairies**, swam, and played together. By the time they were three, Pa Thorpe had taught his boys to ride a horse. He showed them how to shoot a bow, set a trap, and hunt. Jim took to it all like a catfish takes to a creek. Although small, he was quick and tough. He was so fast and had so much **endurance** that he could run down a rabbit on foot. When it came to the old ways, those skills that made the men of the Sac and Fox great providers for their families, Jim was a great learner. By the time the twins were six, Pa Thorpe said Jim knew more about the woods than many men.

The Sac and Fox Nation

The Sac and Fox nation is a **confederacy** of two tribes, the Sauk and the Mesquakie, originally based in eastern Michigan and northern Ohio. By the late eighteenth century, they lived mostly in southern Wisconsin and northern Illinois. Their large village of Saukenuk,

A map of what is now known as Rock Island, Illinois. The clustered black dots show the area occupied by the village of Saukenuk, while the other labels show contemporary names.

located where the Mississippi and Rock Rivers meet, was described by an English traveler in 1766 as "the largest and best-built Indian town." Surrounded by hundreds of acres of planted fields, its population was estimated to be as high as 6,000.

In their own language, the Sauk called themselves the Asakiwaki, or "People of the Outlet." This was eventually shortened in English to Sac. The Mesquakie, or "Red Earth People," became known to the French as "Renards," the French word for foxes. Apparently, when early French visitors asked a group of Mesquakies to identify themselves, they replied that they were Wahgohagi, or members of the Fox Clan. Thus their **clan** name was mistaken for the name of their **tribal nation.**

Closely related in language and culture, the Sauk and Mesquakie thrived, intermarried, and gained a reputation as a powerful nation to be feared by their enemies. But by the beginning of the 19th century, the balance of power between American Indians and Europeans was beginning to change. In 1803, the **Louisiana Purchase** opened up vast new lands for

An 1838 image of Keokuk by a Philadelphia artist (who may never have seen him).

American expansion to the west. The idea of **"manifest destiny"** began to dominate United States policy. Settlers poured into Native lands between the Ohio River and the Mississippi, resulting in an Indian armed resistance that lasted for several decades.

The solution that the US government applied to

the Sac and Fox was the one used to solve nearly all "Indian problems," namely: Get rid of the Indians. After the conclusion of the **Black Hawk War** in 1832, Keokuk, the principal chief of the Sac and Fox, convinced his people to give up their Wisconsin, Illinois, and Iowa lands—more than ten million acres—and move to a 435,000-acre **reservation** in what is now Kansas.

In Kansas, the Sac and Fox found themselves intruding on the traditional hunting grounds of powerful plains tribes, all of whom **resented** the new "frontier Indians." The Sac and Fox were good at fighting, but still, their numbers **dwindled**. Two thousand four hundred people had been settled on the Kansas reservation under the Treaty of 1842. Within twenty years, half of their population had died of disease.

Meanwhile, the United States broke its treaty with the Sac and Fox. In 1854, Congress passed the **Kansas-Nebraska Act**, which stated that the Indians of the region should be resettled in the region then known as Indian Territory (now the state of Oklahoma). Five years later, a group of Sac and Fox leaders signed a

Keokuk's son and grandson—Watchful Fox
(also known as Moses Keokuk) and fourteen-
year-old Charles Keokuk—taken during an
1868 trip to Washington, D.C.

new treaty in which they gave up 300,000 acres of their

Kansas reservation. In 1866 they were pressured to

give up the rest of their land in Kansas in exchange for

money they could use to buy land in Indian Territory.

In December of 1869, during a heavy snowstorm,

the survivors of what had once been a mighty nation

made their last relocation. The remaining Sac and Fox people—as few as 387 by one count—made the nineteen-day trek to Indian Territory. There, on about 480,000 acres of land, less than 10 percent of which was suitable for farming, they received a yearly payment of $60 each. There, in Indian Territory, Jim Thorpe would be born eighteen years later.

The Sac and Fox nation still exists today, with more than 3,700 **tribally enrolled** members headquartered in Stroud, Oklahoma.

CHAPTER TWO
THE AGENCY BOARDING SCHOOL

Their sixth year brought a big change for Jim and Charlie. The Indian Agency that oversaw the reservation said that when Sac and Fox children reached age six, they had to go to the Agency Boarding School. Indian boarding schools did not provide the same education offered to whites. Indian children were educated only to be maids or laborers. In addition, the boarding schools were designed to cut them off from everything that made them Indians—their language, their traditions, even their families— and make them fit in with white society.

Jim's father had become one of the few Sac

and Fox men who could read and write English. He'd seen uneducated Indians cheated out of everything by dishonest men who tricked the Indians into signing papers they could not read.

"My sons," he said to Jim and Charlie, "you need white man's knowledge to survive."

It was no surprise that Jim hated school. He had to wear awful clothes—a heavy wool suit, a felt cap, tight shoes, a shirt and necktie that strangled him. He also got smacked hard across his knuckles with a wooden ruler whenever he spoke a word of Sac. He missed Ma's cooking and Pa's stories about their clan an-cestor, Chief Black

Hawk, the famous warrior who had fought the whites to defend his people. Worst of all, school kept Jim inside all day and locked him up all night in a cold **dormitory** away from the forest and prairies. It made him feel like a fox caught in an iron trap. Jim didn't care about what school might do for him or his people. He just wanted to get away from it.

Charlie was better at his studies than Jim. He didn't seem to mind the **military discipline**

or being stuck at a desk. Solving an arithmetic problem was a challenge to Charlie the way winning a race was to Jim. Now it was Charlie who was waiting for his brother to catch up.

"Come on, Jim," Charlie said. "Don't give up. You can do it."

So, Jim tried to master basic arithmetic, reading, and writing. Then, in his third year of school, something happened that broke his heart.

Black Hawk

Jim Thorpe's ancestor Black Hawk was known also as Ma-ka-tai-me-she-kia-kiak, or Black Sparrow Hawk. Born in 1767 in the Saukenuk village of Rock River, near what is present-day Rock Island, Illinois, Black Hawk was not a **hereditary civil** chief. Instead, like his father, Pyesa, who was the tribal **medicine man** of the Sac people, he gained status as a "war chief" or, more correctly, a "war captain" from his successes in battle. When his father was killed in a raid against the Cherokees, Black Hawk inherited his **medicine bundle,** which further enhanced his status as a war leader.

Many Natives wanted to fight the American takeover of Native lands. Tecumseh (1768–1813) of the Shawnee forged an intertribal alliance that included Black Hawk and some of his fellow Sac and Fox warriors, but Tecumseh's power was broken in 1811 by the American army at the Battle of Tippecanoe. During the **War of 1812,** Black Hawk led a band of about two hundred Sac warriors who allied themselves with the British against

Black Hawk in 1833.

the Americans. Colonel Robert Dickson, the Englishman chosen to bring together the various allies from numerous tribes, placed Black Hawk in command over all of the Native tribal fighters. After the Americans won the war, Black Hawk continued to resist their invasion of Sac and Fox lands, even as another Sac and Fox chief, Keokuk, the "Watchful Fox," gave in to demands to abandon the large village of Saukenuk and move the tribe to Iowa. Finally, in 1831, Black Hawk and a band of followers agreed to leave Saukenuk and accept Keokuk as chief. Black Hawk was 65 years old at the time and had been fighting for most of his life.

But then a prophet named White Cloud from the Winnebago (now Ho-Chunk) tribe urged Black Hawk to resist the Americans and reclaim his lands. A band of Fox warriors came to him for sanctuary. Followers from other nations, Kickapoos and Potawatomis, joined Black Hawk's band. When the spring of 1832 came, Black Hawk led a group of over 2,000 men, women and children back to Saukenuk.

This was the beginning of the tragic **misadventure** that became known as the Black Hawk War. Keokuk had warned the Americans of Black Hawk's plans. A large force of federal troops and Illinois volunteers were sent to stop him. (Among them was a lanky 23-year-old from New Salem, Illinois: Abraham Lincoln, who would later become the 16th president of the United States.) Black Hawk led his followers north, seeking support from other Native nations with no success. Some—among them the Menominees, Winnebagos, and Sioux— joined forces with the Americans to fight against him.

On May 14, Black Hawk found himself facing **cavalry** under US Major Isaiah Stillman and 275 **militiamen**. It seemed hopeless, so he sent a party to Stillman under a flag of truce. Despite the white flag, the troops attacked and killed three Indians. Black Hawk and his warriors then made a stand so fierce that the militiamen panicked and took flight back to a town twenty-five miles away. "Stillman's Run," as it became

In this 1876 picture of the Battle of Bad Axe, women and children make their way to the river as warriors fight in the background.

known, was the only real Indian victory of the campaign. From then on, it was fight, flight, and hunger for Black Hawk's desperate followers.

The Black Hawk War ended on August 3, 1832, when the starving, tattered band reached the **junction** of the Mississippi with the Bad Axe River in what is now Wisconsin. Black Hawk tried again to talk with the Americans, and as before, his **envoys** were fired upon. Hundreds of others then tried to flee across the river in canoes and on **makeshift** rafts. They were cut down by heavy fire from the shore and a gunboat on the river. Only thirty-nine women and children survived. Black Hawk, White Cloud, and a number of their followers were taken prisoner. In 1833, Keokuk arranged for the release of most of the prisoners, but Black Hawk and four others were judged too dangerous to set free. They were sent to another prison in Maryland.

In the east, Black Hawk and the other prisoners were treated as celebrities. Their tragic war was already becoming a part of the American **mythology** of the West. They met President Andrew Jackson, who was surprisingly friendly. They were given new clothing. In May, their promises to end all resistance resulted in their release. They were taken on a tour of Eastern cities, where people **gawked** at them and gave them presents. Near the end of their tour, properly awed by the wealth and power of the Americans, Black Hawk made this statement to a group of Seneca Indians: "Brothers, we have seen how great a people the Whites are. They are very rich and very strong—it is folly for us to fight them."

He allowed himself to be taken to the new Sac and Fox reservation in Iowa, where he died in 1838. With the exception of the Seminole resistance in Florida, Black Hawk's War marked the end of armed conflict between the United States and the tribes east of the Mississippi.

CHAPTER THREE

JIM ALONE

Sickness often struck the crowded, unheated dormitories of the Indian boarding schools. **Sanitation** was poor, and there were no real doctors to tend the sick. **Epidemics** of influenza swept through like prairie fires. Even common childhood diseases such as measles and whooping cough could be fatal to the Indian children jammed together in those schools.

Charlie was one of those who became sick. He caught pneumonia and died. Jim felt as if the sunlight had gone from his life. His twin brother had been his best friend.

Jim's mother tried to comfort her son, but he was **inconsolable**. He would never hear

Charlie's encouraging voice again. The thought of going back to school without his brother tore at Jim's heart.

"Let me work around the farm, Pa," Jim begged.

His father, though, was sure he knew what was best.

"Son," he said, "you have to get an education.

Charlie would have wanted you to keep learning."

Jim tried to listen to his father, but when he returned to school and saw the empty cot where Charlie had slept, it was too much for him. As soon as the teacher's back was turned, Jim ran the twenty-three miles back home, straight as an arrow.

Pa Thorpe had no choice but to send his stubborn son even farther away. So young Jim, at age eleven, was sent to Haskell Institute in Lawrence, Kansas, almost three hundred miles away.

Haskell was stricter than the Agency Boarding School. There children from more than eighty tribes were dressed in military uniforms and were awakened before dawn with a bugle call. **Manual** training was mixed with

classroom studies to teach them trades useful to white society. Hard work was the rule, and the students of Haskell did it all—growing corn, making bread, building wagons, and sewing their own uniforms.

Jim did better at Haskell. He worked in the engineering shop. Learning how things were made was more interesting than being cooped up in a classroom.

Plus Haskell had something the Agency Boarding School didn't have—football. For the first time in his life, Jim saw a football game. The cheers of the crowd and the athleticism of the players wakened something deep inside Jim, the same emotions that had been stirred by Pa's stories of Black Hawk and the other warriors who had fought for their people. Jim knew right away that football was something he wanted to play.

But Jim was too small for the sport. He was less than five feet tall and weighed just one hundred pounds. He joined the track team instead and became one of the fastest runners. Meanwhile, he watched every football game he could. Jim also met Chauncy Archiquette, Haskell's best football player, who taught him about the game. Chauncy even helped Jim make a little football out of scrap leather stuffed with rags. With that football, Jim organized games with other boys too small for the school team.

How Football Started

American football can trace its origins back to soccer and rugby, games first played in England. Soccer is called "football" everywhere except in North America. Only one player in soccer, the goalie, is allowed to touch the ball with his hands. In 1823, schoolboys in England began to change the rules of the game by picking up the ball and carrying it. The new game was named "rugby" after the Rugby School, one of the oldest of England's private schools, where it was first played.

The evolution of rugby-style football in the United States was **chaotic.** An 1869 game between Rutgers and Princeton Universities in New Jersey was the first documented contest between two American colleges in which players carried the ball and actually called their game "football" rather than rugby. Many colleges took up the sport, but because each college made up its own rules, problems soon arose. It became necessary to **standardize** the rules. Thus it was that in

This 1878 print by artist Julian Davidson shows "a game of football." Note the players' "helmets" and uniforms.

1876, representatives from the athletic departments of Harvard, Yale, Columbia, and Princeton Universities met and created the **Intercollegiate** Football Association to **regulate** the game. American football was officially born.

A Yale student named Walter Camp, who attended the meeting, loved the new game of football. In 1888, just six years after he graduated from Yale, he became the university's head football coach and eventually the athletic director. Camp edited every American football rulebook until his death in 1925. Among the **innovations** that he introduced were eleven-man teams (instead of fifteen); the establishment of a **line of scrimmage** separating the two teams before each play; the quarterback and center positions; the forward pass; down and distance rules; tackling below the waist; and the scoring and penalty systems.

Glenn Scobey Warner (a.k.a. "Pop"), who would serve as Jim Thorpe's coach, was another important innovator and **strategist** of the game. He invented the technique of **body blocking** and many plays and formations, as well as the **three-point stance.** He is also famous for plays and tricks that were soon outlawed. They included sewing a football-shaped leather patch to the front of players' uniforms to make it hard to tell who had the ball; running off the field behind the opposing team's bench and then coming back on to catch a pass downfield; and a play called the "hunchback," in which the ball was shoved inside the ball carrier's shirt.

American college football rapidly gained popularity. The first college football league, an early version of the **Big Ten,** was founded in 1895. In 1902, Michigan beat Stanford 49–0 in the first post-season game, the Rose Bowl. At the same time, football was an incredibly violent game. Records indicate that there were either eighteen or nineteen deaths in college football in 1905. President Theodore Roosevelt publicly voiced his opinion that the game should be banned unless changes were made. As a result, sixty-two schools

The 1902 Rose Bowl Game.

joined to form the Intercollegiate Athletic Association, to devise rules and practices that would make the game safer. Later the Association was renamed the National Collegiate Athletic Association (NCAA), which survives to this day.

CHAPTER FOUR
WHAT AN INDIAN CAN DO

Near the end of his second year at Haskell, Jim got word that his father had been shot in a hunting accident and was dying. Jim's only thought was that he had to get home. He ran off and headed south. It took him two weeks to reach their farm. To his surprise, Pa was there, recovered from his wound and waiting.

"We knew you were coming home," his father said, embracing him.

Jim never returned to Haskell. Shortly after he returned home, his mother died of a sudden illness. Jim grieved over the loss of his mother, and Pa Thorpe finally agreed that his son did not have to go back to boarding school.

Jim's father believed his son still needed education, so Jim began attending school nearby in Garden Grove. At Garden Grove, students were learning about a new thing called electricity. Electricity could make it seem as if the sun were still shining, even at night. The thought of that appealed to Jim. Electrical sunlight could be brought to Indian homes too. Pa Thorpe had always told Jim that education would give him the ability to help his people. Maybe becoming an electrician was the bright path he was supposed to follow.

One day a **recruiter** from the Carlisle Indian School in Pennsylvania came to Garden Grove. Carlisle was always looking for Indian students who were good athletes, and the recruiter had heard of Jim's success as a runner at Haskell.

"Would you like to be a Carlisle man?" the recruiter asked.

"Can I study electricity there?" Jim said.

"Of course," the recruiter replied, even though Carlisle offered no such course.

Something else also attracted Jim to Carlisle—sports. Carlisle was one of the first and most well-known of the Indian boarding schools. Everyone knew about the school and its amazing record of winning sports teams. The Carlisle Indians even beat teams from the big, famous colleges. At Carlisle, Jim thought, he could play football.

Pa Thorpe urged Jim to seize the opportunity. Somehow he knew Carlisle would be the first step on a trail that would lead his son to greatness.

"Son," he said, "you are an Indian. I want you to show other races what an Indian can do."

Soon after Jim arrived at Carlisle, he received bad news. His father had been bitten by a snake while working in his fields and had died of blood poisoning. The man who had fought so hard to force his son to get an education was gone.

Carlisle and Other Indian Boarding Schools

Formal classroom education was not new to Native Americans of the 1800s. Both white and Indian teachers, many of them missionaries, had long provided Western education to various tribes, and many tribal leaders thought the same way Jim Thorpe's father did: They believed that if their children gained a white education, they could use that knowledge to help protect their fellow Indians. But in the late nineteenth century, education became a weapon against the survival of Indian cultures with the creation of Indian boarding schools.

The best known of these institutions was the Indian Industrial School in Carlisle, Pennsylvania, headed by Richard Henry Pratt. While serving in the US Army, Pratt discovered that he could work well with Indian scouts, and gradually came to the conclusion that color and race were **artificial** barriers between people. Any man, Pratt realized, could better himself. "The rights of citizenship," he wrote, "include equal **fraternity** and

Richard Henry Pratt in 1890.

equal **privilege** for development." It was a **radical** idea for his time, and he would pursue it passionately for the rest of his life.

In 1875, Pratt was given the job of escorting seventy-two Indian prisoners to St. Augustine, Florida. As their jailer, Pratt saw an opportunity to try out some of his new ideas. He gave his charges considerable freedom, dressed them in military uniforms, and treated them as new recruits. He also began offering classes in reading, writing, and Bible study.

The results, Pratt would later claim, were that his men "set an example to civilization in good behavior." Not only did they learn to read and write, several went on to further education. His successes were not without some setbacks, but Pratt was now convinced he had found the way to solve the nation's so-called "Indian Problem": The Indian needed to be raised to the level of white culture.

This idea would now be called **patronizing** and **ethnocentric**. But while Pratt respected Native intelligence and potential, he felt that Native cultures held Natives back. He developed a plan for "civilizing" Indian children. Native children taken far away from their homes and placed in a **regimented** setting could more readily be forced to leave behind the traditional lifestyle of their relatives on the reservations.

Pratt **acquired** an abandoned military **barracks** in Carlisle, Pennsylvania, for his experiment. The Carlisle Indian Industrial School opened in 1879, and became the model for two dozen other schools around the nation, including Haskell Institute in Kansas. Boarding and day schools also grew up near most of the reservations, such as the Sac and Fox school where Jim was first cooped up in a classroom.

During the thirty-nine years Carlisle was open, more than ten thousand children from dozens of tribes attended the school. Many of them started when they were very young, and they were separated from their families for at least five years. On arrival at Carlisle, the boys had their long hair cut and were dressed in military uniforms. The girls were outfitted in **drab** dresses and taught to wear their hair in Western fashion. All students were forbidden to speak their tribal language or engage in any traditional practices. Strict penalties, including jail time and beatings, were **meted** out to offenders. Students were required to go to church on Sunday and trained in such useful skills as sewing and carpentry, leatherwork, farming, and baking, in addition to reading, writing, and arithmetic. Painting, debating, poetry, and the plays of Shakespeare were considered important parts of a well-rounded education.

Vocational training and manual labor were highly stressed at all the Indian boarding schools. It was strongly believed that training in useful trades would give Indians the best chance to earn a living after leaving school and entering the workforce. (Many teachers also wrongly believed that Indians lacked the mental abilities to succeed in any vocational training other than simple labor.) Carlisle and the other Indian schools also relied heavily on the unpaid work of their students, who did the cooking, the laundry, the groundskeeping, and all the other jobs needed to keep a school running smoothly and in good repair. For example, when **steam heat** was introduced to the campus buildings,

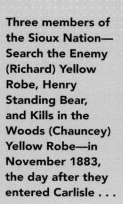

Three members of the Sioux Nation—Search the Enemy (Richard) Yellow Robe, Henry Standing Bear, and Kills in the Woods (Chauncey) Yellow Robe—in November 1883, the day after they entered Carlisle . . .

it was Indian students who dug the trenches and fit the pipes.

The Outing System at Carlisle was an important part of the school's training. In order to give the students a sense of the working world and to place them in white families, who were supposed to accept them into their households, many Carlisle students were sent out to labor in outlying farms and shops at very low wages. Some were also sent to work in factories,

. . . and in November 1886, after three years at the school.

including the Ford plant in Detroit, Michigan, in the 1910s. Many of the outing students were treated well, but others suffered neglect and abuse at the hands of their host families. Jim Thorpe's own school record at Carlisle indicates that he was sent off to a farm only four months after his arrival, but that he ran away and came back to Carlisle. He was sent out to yet another farm not long after. During his first three years at the Indian School, Jim spent twenty-one months on farms and only about fourteen months on campus.

Carlisle's reputation was built on its sports program, which was second to none. Although the education of its older students was only at the high school level, and thus the number of Indian athletes old enough and talented enough to engage in college-level sports was quite small, Carlisle's teams began competing with great success against some of the largest and most **prestigious** colleges and universities, including the **Ivy League** teams of Harvard, Yale, and the University of Pennsylvania. It helped, of course, that Carlisle employees recruited talented and promising American

Calisle plays Yale in football, October 24, 1896.

Indian athletes from all over the United States. Initially opposed to football because of its violence, Pratt later accepted and celebrated it because it enhanced the image of his school.

Carlisle's overall record was far from perfect. Fewer than a thousand Indian students actually graduated. More than a thousand ran away. Children suffered from homesickness, disease, and abuse at the school. The Carlisle cemetery is full of the graves of Indian children who died there. Others, sent home suffering from one epidemic disease or another, not only died at home but passed their sickness on to others in their communities.

Communities and families were also affected in another way. The harsh military discipline of Carlisle (and most other Indian schools) stood in sharp contrast to the warm family atmosphere Indian children usually enjoyed at home. After being raised in these institutions, many Indian boarding school students found it hard to become loving and **nurturing** parents when they returned to their tribal nations. They had been cut off from the training critical to their traditional identity, relative to family, extended family, and nation.

A postcard showing the Carlisle campus in 1914.

There were other problems as well, even for Carlisle's success stories. Those who **"assimilated"** still found little opportunity to succeed in white society, where they were often viewed as "savages." They also found it hard to fit in when they eventually returned home—strangers in their own lands, caught between two worlds. One way or another, every American Indian family in the United States was affected by the boarding schools, which persisted well into the second half of the twentieth century. While most schools closed

Panoramic View of Indian School and Campus, Carlisle, Pa.

in the 1980s, the US government's Bureau of Indian Education still runs a few off-reservation boarding high schools, which American Indian teenagers can choose to attend. These schools now encourage cultural education and exploration, and students can study traditional Native languages and crafts.

CHAPTER FIVE
AT CARLISLE

Already a quiet person, Jim retreated further into silence after his father's death. But he did not **desert** Carlisle. Perhaps Jim felt the best way to remember his father was to live the dream Pa Thorpe had for him. It was now up to Jim to push himself.

The Carlisle system of sending new students off campus for work experience helped. Jim ended up at a farm in New Jersey. The farm labor reminded him of the many hours he had spent working by Pa's side in Oklahoma. Jim worked so hard and with such quiet confidence that everyone saw him as a man they could like and trust. To his delight, Jim was made foreman, head of all the workers.

When Jim came back to Carlisle in the fall, he was no longer a boy. He had grown taller, stronger, more self-assured. He was ready to play football, but he knew it would not be easy. Carlisle's famous coach Pop Warner would only

allow the best to join his track squad or his football team as one of his "Athletic Boys."

One day Jim's big chance came. He was on his way to play a game of **scrub football** with some of his friends who were too small for the school team. As Jim crossed the field, he saw a group of **varsity** athletes practicing the high jump.

Jim asked if he could have a try, even though he was wearing overalls and an old pair of work shoes. The Athletic Boys **snickered** as they reset the bar for him. They placed it higher than anyone at Carlisle had ever jumped. Even in his work clothes, Jim cleared the bar on his first jump. No one could believe it. People stood around with their mouths wide open, staring. Jim just grinned and walked off to play football with his friends.

The next day Jim was told to report to the office of Coach Warner. Everyone knew Pop Warner was a great coach, but he was also a man with a bad temper. Jim wondered if Pop was going to yell at him for interrupting track practice.

"Do you know what you've done?" Pop Warner growled.

"Nothing bad, I hope," Jim said.

"Bad?" Pop Warner said. His face broke into a smile. "Boy, you've just broken the school record. Go down to the clubhouse and exchange those overalls for a track outfit. You're on my track team now."

Glenn Scobey "Pop" Warner

Glenn Scobey "Pop" Warner was born in 1871 in Springville, Illinois. Although he loved playing baseball and football as a boy, his coaching career began almost by accident. After working from 1889 to 1892 on the ranch his family purchased in Texas, Warner returned to Springville. Almost as soon as he got there, he lost all his money gambling on horse races. Though uninterested in attending college, he told his father he needed money to go to school to become a lawyer. With the $100 his father gave him, he enrolled at Cornell University. There he rediscovered his love for sports, playing from 1892 to 1894 as a guard on the school's football team. Because he was in his twenties and slightly older than most of the other players, he was given the nickname of "Pop." He became the school heavyweight boxing champion, but a shoulder injury prevented him from playing his favorite sport, which was baseball.

After college, Warner turned his mind to football, a

Pop Warner circa 1915.

sport then in its infancy, and got his first coaching job at what is now Iowa State University. One of the greatest innovators in the history of the game, he invented many techniques, plays, and blocking schemes still in use today. After coaching at Georgia and Cornell, he came to Carlisle in 1899, where he created a football program that would dominate the nation for much of his tenure there, from 1899–1903 and 1907–1914. He also coached the Carlisle track squad, and went to the Olympics with his Native American athletes in 1912, where Jim Thorpe won gold. Warner controlled all the money that came into Carlisle due to its athletic successes. He also acted as Jim's agent for Major League Baseball. After he negotiated a $6,500 contract for Jim with the New York Giants—a huge sum at that time— Warner took home a fee of $2,500.

Warner went on to coach at Pittsburgh, Stanford, Temple, and San Jose State. His career as a head football coach spanned four decades, as he retired in 1938 with a record of 319–106–32, among the best in the history of the game. He also helped form the popular national youth football program later named after him: Pop Warner Little Scholars. Warner was one of the first coaches inducted into the College Football Hall of Fame in 1951. He passed away at his home in Palo Alto, California, in 1954, at the age of 83.

CHAPTER SIX
STAR ATHLETE

Before long Jim Thorpe was Carlisle's best track athlete. He competed in the high jump, the hurdles, and the dashes, winning or placing in all of them. Still, Jim wanted to play football. Reluctantly, Pop Warner told him he could give it a try.

Pop Warner didn't like the idea of his slender high jumper being injured in a football game, so he decided to discourage Jim by beginning his first practice with a tackling drill. Jim, the newcomer, had to take the ball and try to run from one end to the other, through the whole varsity team.

"Is that all?" Jim said. He looked at the football

in his hands. It was the first time he'd ever held a real football, but he believed in himself. Then he took off down the field like a deer. He was past half the team before the players even saw him coming. At the other end Jim looked back. Behind him was the whole Carlisle team, the players holding nothing in their hands but air. There was a grin on Jim's face when he handed Coach Warner the ball.

"Doggone it," Pop Warner said. "You're supposed to give the first team tackling practice, not run through them." Pop Warner slammed the ball back into Jim's belly. "Do it again."

Jim's jaw was set as he ran the Carlisle **gauntlet** a second time. He was carrying not just a football, but the hopes and dreams of his family, his people, and all the Indians who had been told they could never compete with the white man. Tacklers bounced off Jim as he lowered his shoulders. No one stopped him. The sun shone around him as he stood in the end zone.

For years Jim had fought against his education. He had run away from it so many times. This time Jim used all he had learned from his mother's wisdom, his brother's encouragement, and his father's fierce determination that his son show what an Indian could do. From now on Jim Thorpe would run forward, toward the finish line, toward the goal. He didn't know how far he would go, but he believed in his journey. His education had put his feet on the bright path.

CHAPTER SEVEN
ALL AMERICAN

That day, on the football field at Carlisle, a legend was born. The quiet American Indian boy from Oklahoma went on to international fame, and Jim Thorpe is now widely acknowledged as the dominant sports figure of the twentieth century.

At Carlisle, Jim not only played football and ran track, he played **lacrosse**, was captain of the basketball team, and was the school's best tennis and **handball** player. His career there spanned six years, broken by a two-year stretch during which he played minor league baseball in North Carolina. That early **foray** into semiprofessional baseball, during which Jim pitched and played first base, would later come back to haunt him.

Jim Thorpe's two greatest college football years were 1911 and 1912. Starting on both offense and defense, he was also the team's kicker and leading tackler. On November 23, 1912, in the Springfield game, Jim scored all thirty of Carlisle's points, and at the end of the 1912 season, he was named an **All American** for the second year in a row. He continued to **excel** in track as well, setting collegiate records in thirteen different events. Although all Jim's records were eventually broken, no one had ever dominated as many events at one time. In fact, it seemed as if Jim could master any sport. He was an excellent golfer and bowler and a superior swimmer, billiards player, figure skater, gymnast, rower, and hockey player.

In 1912, coached by Pop Warner, Jim Thorpe went to the Olympic Games in Stockholm, Sweden. There he won both the **pentathlon** and the **decathlon.** After placing the laurel wreath on Jim's head and handing him the gold medals, the king of Sweden extended his hand.

"Sir," King Gustav said, "you are the greatest athlete in the world."

Jim took his hand and shook it. "Thanks, King," he said.

Jim Thorpe had truly shown the world what

an Indian could do. But sadly, in 1913, Jim's glory at the Olympics was spoiled by the **disclosure** that he had played minor league baseball in 1909 and 1910. When asked if this was true, Jim freely admitted it. Many other college athletes did the same in those days, and Jim thought he had done nothing wrong. But only **amateur** athletes, who

had never been paid for their participation in any sport, were allowed to compete in the Olympics at that time.

Pop Warner denied knowing anything about Jim's baseball career, but documents from Carlisle tell another story. Thorpe's official school record states plainly that he was "granted a summer leave to play baseball in the South." As the evidence of Jim's professional play mounted, Warner realized he could be ruined if people learned he had knowingly sponsored a professional athlete at the Stockholm Olympics.

There was only one way out. Warner and the superintendent of Carlisle wrote a letter in which Jim "confessed" to deceiving his coach and everyone else because he was "simply an Indian school boy" and did not know he was doing wrong. Other members of the Carlisle team urged Thorpe not to go along with it, but he remained loyal to Coach Warner and did as he was told.

The Amateur Athletic Union ruled that as a professional, Jim should not have competed in the Olympics. Although the International Olympic Committee did not ask for the return of Thorpe's medals, Pop Warner was holding them "in safekeeping" for Jim, and he packed them up and returned them to the Committee. Jim was stripped of his amateur status, and his name was removed from the Olympic record books.

CHAPTER EIGHT
A LASTING LEGACY

Jim Thorpe went on to a great and varied career in professional sports. When he left college, he became a professional baseball player, and from 1913 to 1919 he played with the New York Giants, the Cincinnati Reds, and the Boston Braves. The big-time era of football began in 1915, when the professional game was reorganized. The Canton Bulldogs scored a publicity **coup** when they signed Jim Thorpe, by then the world's best-known American Indian as well as the world's most famous athlete.

Jim led Canton to victory game after game, including three unofficial world champion-ships. When the American Professional Football

Association (later known as the National Football League) was formed in 1920, the members elected Jim Thorpe president. President or not, Jim kept playing until 1929 for teams including the New York Giants and the Oorang Indians. By age forty-two, even Jim was too old for pro football, and he retired.

Jim Thorpe was a determined but gentle person with a great sense of humor and an un-forgettable grin, a modest man whose greatest virtue was his love of honesty. He gave inspiring lectures around the country about his career and the importance of providing equal rights and opportunities for American Indians. "I would like to ask every one of you here to work for the improvement of Indian conditions," Jim would often say at the end of his talks. His **eloquent** words affected the lives of countless people, who held him up as a fine example of what an Indian could do.

Married three times, Jim Thorpe had five

sons and three daughters. After his death in 1953, his children tried to follow his example of fighting for Indian rights. His daughter Grace, an activist with the National Congress of American Indians, also devoted herself to ensuring that her father's athletic accomplishments would not be forgotten. Through her efforts and those of many others, the Amateur Athletic Union restored Jim's status as an amateur and the International Olympic Committee reversed its decision in 1982. In 1983, duplicate gold medals were given to the Thorpe family. Jim Thorpe's path was bright again.

Jim Thorpe in 1912.

AUTHOR'S NOTE

My inspiration to write a book for young readers about Jim Thorpe came from two people and two songs. The first was Swift Eagle, an Apache/Pueblo elder who worked with Jim in Hollywood. Swifty started me thinking about this project more than twenty years ago when he taught me a song Jim Thorpe had given him in 1935. The second was my good friend and fellow former athlete Jack Gladstone, a Blackfeet folk singer. Jack's wonderful song about Jim, "Bright Path," was and remains an inspiration to me.

It is also important to recognize that many people worked very hard over the years to pass on Jim Thorpe's legacy and restore the Olympic medals that were taken from him. None deserve more credit than his children, especially his daughter Grace Thorpe. Like her father, she has been a strong voice for Native American rights. I deeply appreciate the help she gave me.

Of all the books written about Jim Thorpe, the best picture of this unique American Indian hero's life is found in Robert L. Whitman's *Jim Thorpe, Athlete of the Century: A Pictorial Biography*. I express my sincere gratitude to Bob for his advice and critical input.

Thanks, too, to Barbara Landis of the Carlisle Historical Society for her suggestions and for sharing back issues of the Carlisle Indian School newsletter, *The Indian Helper*. There are still so many true stories that need to be told about the victories won by Indian children who tried their best, against unimaginable odds, at schools such as Carlisle. I just hope this book is worthy of them and their families, of Jim Thorpe and his family, and of all those—past, present, and future—touched by his great life.

TIMELINE

* Marks a date obtained from Thorpe family or most reliable sources

1887* May 28: James Francis Thorpe and twin brother, Charles, born on Sac and Fox Indian Reservation along North Canadian River in Oklahoma

1893 Enters Agency Boarding School with Charlie

1896 Charlie dies of pneumonia

1898 Arrives at Haskell Institute in Lawrence, Kansas

1902* Charlotte Thorpe (mother) dies; begins attending school in Garden Grove, Oklahoma

1904 Enters United States Indian Industrial School in Carlisle, Pennsylvania; Hiram Thorpe (father) dies

1907-1912 Plays college football

1909-1910 Plays minor league baseball

1911, 1912 Named First Team All American Halfback at Carlisle

1912 Wins gold medals in pentathlon and decathlon at Olympic Games in Stockholm, Sweden

1913 Stripped of Olympic gold medals and name removed from record books

1913-1919 Plays major league baseball

1915-1929 Plays professional football

1917 Becomes a United States citizen

1920 Elected first president of American Professional Football Association (now National Football League)

1922 Forms Oorang Indians, an all-Indian professional football team

1929 Retires from professional football at age forty-two

1950 Voted America's Greatest Football Player and Greatest All-Around Male Athlete of first half century by Associated Press

1951 World premiere of movie *Jim Thorpe, All American,* starring Burt Lancaster as Thorpe

1953 Dies March 28; buried in Mauch Park, Pennsylvania, which later is renamed Jim Thorpe, Pennsylvania

1958 Elected to National Indian Hall of Fame

1963 Inducted into Pro Football Hall of Fame as part of original class

1973 Amateur Athletic Union reverses 1913 decision and changes Thorpe's status to amateur

1975 Inducted into National Track & Field Hall of Fame

1982 International Olympic Committee restores Thorpe's name to record books

1983 Duplicate Olympic gold medals given to Thorpe family; inducted into US Olympic Hall of Fame

1998 United States Postal Service issues Jim Thorpe commemorative stamp as part of its Celebrate the Century program

1999 Resolution put forth in United States Congress to recognize Thorpe as America's Athlete of the Century

2000 Voted Athlete of the Century by ABC's *Wide World of Sports*

2001 Memorialized on Wheaties® The Breakfast of Champions cereal box

GLOSSARY

acquire (ah-KWI-er) *verb* to get something

All American (awl ah-MAYR-ee-kan) *proper noun* an athletic honor given to players who are considered to be the best in their sport in the entire United States

amateur (AM-uh-chur) *noun* someone who participates in an activity for the fun of it rather than for pay

artificial (art-eh-FISH-el) *adjective* fake

assimilate (ah-SIM-eh-layt) *verb* to absorb a thing and make it similar to the rest

barracks (BARE-ax) *noun* a building or group of buildings used to house soldiers

Big Ten (big ten) *proper noun* the oldest collegiate athletic conference in the United States, founded in 1895, traditionally including large universities in the upper Midwest

Black Hawk War (blak hawk wor) *proper noun* a conflict lasting from April to August 1832 between the United States government and a band of Sac, Fox, and Kickapoo Indians

body blocking (BAH-dee BLAHK-ing) *noun* a technique in American football where defenders try to stop the advance of offensive players by blocking them with their shoulders or chests

cavalry (KA-vahl-ree) *noun* a group of soldiers mounted on horseback

chaotic (KAY-ah-tik) *adjective* messy, disorganized

civil (SIV-ul) *adjective* of or relating to citizens or the state

clan (klan) *noun* in a Native American context, a group of extended family members within a larger tribe or nation

confederacy (kun-FED-er-uh-see) *noun* an alliance among a group of people or organizations

coup (koo) *noun* a significant accomplishment, often an unexpected one

decathlon (dee-KATH-a-lon) *noun* an athletic contest consisting of ten different challenges

desert (deh-ZURT) *verb* to abandon

discipline (DIS-uh-plen) *noun* punishment, or any form of training that drills a student in "right" behavior

disclosure (dis-KLOW-zure) *noun* uncovering; revelation

dormitory (DOOR-meh-toor-ee) *noun* a building where people sleep

drab (drab) *adjective* colorless or dull

dwindle (DWIN-dell) *noun* to steadily reduce in size

eloquent (EH-low-kwent) *adjective* having a smooth and effective speaking style

endurance (en-DOOR-ents) *noun* the ability to withstand pain or hardship

envoy (AHN-voy) *noun* one who carries a message, especially a government official

epidemic (eh-puh-DEH-mik) *noun* outbreak of disease that spreads very quickly and affects a large number of people

ethnocentric (ehth-no-SEN-trik) *adjective* having a belief in the superiority of one particular ethnic group

excel (ek-SELL) *verb* to be excellent, especially in comparison to others

foray (FOR-ay) *noun* an effort to explore a new area of action

fraternity (frah-TUR-neh-tee) *noun* brotherhood

gauntlet (GAWNT-let) *noun* a line of people who try to strike or stop another person running by or through them

gawk (gawk) *verb* to stare

handball (HAND-boll) *noun* a game played by two people hitting a ball against a wall with their hands

hereditary (huh-REH-dee-tare-ee) *adjective* received through an inheritance from one's family

inconsolable (in-kon-SO-luh-bull) *adjective* unable to be comforted

innovation (IN-no-vay-shun) *noun* a new idea or way to do something

intercollegiate (in-ter-kol-LEE-jit) *adjective* shared between or among colleges

Ivy League (AYE-vee LEE-guh) *proper noun* a confederacy of eight prestigious colleges located in the northeastern United States

junction (JUNK-shun) *noun* a meeting point

Kansas-Nebraska Act (KAN-zas nee-BRAH-skuh akt) *proper noun* an 1854 law that created the Kansas and Nebraska territories, opening them to official United States colonization and settlement

lacrosse (la-KROSS) *noun* a sport originated by the Iroquois people of New York and Pennsylvania, where team members throw and catch balls using a small net on a stick

line of scrimmage (lyne ov SKRIM-muj) *noun* in football, an imaginary line that teams cannot cross until a new play begins

Louisiana Purchase (loo-ee-zee-AN-na) *proper noun* an 1803 agreement in which the United States bought more than 800,000 square miles of land from France, including all or parts of what is now Louisiana, Texas, Oklahoma, Arkansas, Missouri, Kansas, Colorado, Wyoming, Nebraska, Iowa, Minnesota, North Dakota, South Dakota, and Montana

makeshift (MAYK-shift) *adjective* something that temporarily fills in for a thing of better quality

manifest destiny (MA-neh-fest DES-ten-ee) *proper noun* in the 1800s, the racist belief that it was the United States's right and fate to settle the entire North American continent

manual (MAN-yoo-ell) *adjective* done with the hands

medicine bundle (MEH-dee-sin BUN-dell) *noun* in some Native American cultures, a wrapped collection of objects with powerful religious and healing properties

medicine man (MEH-dee-sin man) *noun* a person in many Native American tribes who served as a priest and healer. Women could also serve as "medicine women"

mete (meet) *verb* to give out or deliver

military (MILL-uh-tayr-ee) *adjective* having to do with soldiers or war

militiamen (MILL-ish-uh-men) *plural noun* people who belong to a militia—a group of armed citizens

misadventure (mis-ad-VEN-chur) *noun* a mistake

mythology (mi-THAW-loh-gee) *noun* a collection of legendary stories

nurturing (NUR-chur-ing) *adjective* caring

patronizing (PAY-tro-ny-zing) *adjective* snobby

pentathlon (pent-ATH-a-lon) *noun* an athletic contest consisting of five different challenges

prairie (PRAYR-ee) *noun* a grassland, particularly the rolling hills of the central United States

prestigious (preh-STIJ-us) *adjective* well-respected, impressive

privilege (PRIV-lij) *noun* a special right, as in something that is deserved

radical (RAD-ee-kull) *adjective* extreme, especially in matters relating to politics

recruiter (ree-KROOT-er) *noun* a person who finds new people to join a particular group

regimented (REJ-ee-mint-ed) *adjective* operating in a rigid manner, similar to the rules of a military unit

regulate (REH-gyew-late) *verb* to create rules for something

resent (REE-zent) *verb* to dislike or be irritated by something

reservation (reh-zer-VAY-shun) *noun* an area of land set aside for a specific purpose; here, the land that the United States government forced Native peoples to move to and stay on from the nineteenth century to the present

sanitation (san-ee-TAY-shun) *noun* condition of cleanliness

scrub football (skrub FOOT-ball) *noun* an informal game of football

snickered (SNIK-erd) *verb* to laugh softly, usually in a mocking way

standardize (STAN-der-dyz) *verb* to take a varied group of things and make them all alike

steam heat (steem heet) *noun* a heating system where heat is created by boiling water in a large tank in the basement and sending the steam up through pipes to individual spaces

strategist (STRAH-tee-jist) *noun* a person who develops a plan to achieve a goal

three-point stance (three poynt stans) *noun* a body position used primarily on the line of scrimmage in a football game, where players put one hand on the ground and bend their knees forward into a high squat, readying them to respond to the next play

tribal nation (TRY-ball NAY-shun) *noun* an independent Native American nation within the United States

tribally enrolled (TRY-ball-ee en-ROLD) *adjective* included in the official listing of a Native American tribe's members

varsity (VAR-seh-tee) *adjective* belonging to the chief competitive team in a sport

vocational (voe-KAY-shun-all) *adjective* related to a specific set of skills

War of 1812 (wor ov 1812) *proper noun* a war fought from June 1812 to February 1815 between the British Empire and the United States

AUTHOR'S SOURCES

Bloom, John. *To Show What an Indian Can Do: Sports at Native American Boarding Schools.* Minneapolis: University of Minnesota Press, 2000.

Bonvillan, Nancy. *The Sac and Fox.* New York: Chelsea House, 1995.

Bruchac, Joseph and Tom Weidlinger. *Jim Thorpe: The World's Greatest Athlete.* Angels Camp, CA: A Moira Productions, 2009.

Buford, Kate. *Native American Son: The Life and Sporting Legend of Jim Thorpe.* Lincoln, NE: University of Nebraska Press, 2010.

Bynum, Mike, ed. *Pop Warner, Football's Greatest Teacher: The Epic Autobiography of Major College Football's Winningest Coach.* Langhorne, PA: Gridiron Properties, 1993.

Cooper, Michael. *Indian School: Teaching the White Man's Way.* New York: Clarion Books, 1999.

Crawford, Bill. *All American: The Rise and Fall of Jim Thorpe.* Hoboken, NJ: John Wiley & Sons, 2005.

Eastman, Ellen Goodale. *Pratt: The Red Man's Moses.* Norman: University of Oklahoma Press, 1935.

Gutman, Allen. *The Olympics: A History of the Modern Games.* Urbana-Champaign: University of Illinois Press, 1992.

Hagan, William T. *The Sac and Fox Indians.* Norman: University of Oklahoma Press, 1958.

Newcombe, Jack. *The Best of the Athletic Boys: The White Man's Impact on Jim Thorpe.* New York: Doubleday, 1975.

Wheeler, Robert L. *Jim Thorpe: World's Greatest Athlete.* Norman: University of Oklahoma Press, 1975.

Whitman, Robert. *Jim Thorpe: Athlete of the Century.* Defiance, OH: The Hubbard Company, 2002.

———. *Jim Thorpe and the Oorang Indians: The N. F. L.'s Most Colorful Franchise.* Mount Vernon, IN: Windmill Publications, 1984.

Witmer, Linda F. *The Indian Industrial School, Carlisle, Pennsylvania, 1879-1918.* Carlisle, PA: Cumberland County Historical Society, 2002.

RECOMMENDED BOOKS, FILMS, AND WEBSITES

Fiction books are marked with an asterisk (*).

THE SAC AND FOX NATION AND BLACK HAWK

Black Hawk. *Autobiography of Ma-ka-tai-me-she-kia-kiak, or Black Hawk.* Rock Island, IL: J. B. Patterson, 1833. https://www.gutenberg.org/files/7097/7097-h/7097-h.htm.The Sac and Fox Nation. http://sacandfoxnation-nsn.gov.

JIM THORPE

Bruchac, Joseph. *Jim Thorpe, Original All-American.* New York: Dial Books/Penguin Random House, 2006.

Coulson, Art. *Unstoppable: How Jim Thorpe and the Carlisle Indian School Football Team Defeated Army.* Illustrated by Nick Hardcastle. North Mankato, MN: Capstone, 2018.

Weidlinger, Tom, dir. *Jim Thorpe: The World's Greatest Athlete.* Angels Camp, CA: Moira Productions, 2009.

HOW FOOTBALL STARTED

Gramling, Gary. *The Football Fanbook*. New York: Time Home Entertainment, 2017.

Jacobs, Greg. *The Everything Kids' Football Book*. Fifth edition. New York: Adams Media, 2016.

Library of Congress and Susan Reyburn. *Football Nation: Four Hundred Years of America's Game*. New York: Harry N. Abrams, 2013.

Revsine, Dave. *The Opening Kickoff: The Tumultuous Birth of a Football Nation*. Guilford, CT: Lyons Press/Globe Pequot Press, 2015.

Sports Illustrated for Kids. *Football: Then to WOW!* New York: Time Home Entertainment, 2014.

INDIAN BOARDING SCHOOLS

* Bruchac, Joseph. *Two Roads*. New York: Dial Books/Penguin Random House, 2018.

Carlisle Indian School Digital Resource Center. Dickinson College. http://carlisleindian.dickinson.edu.

Dupuis, Jenny Kay, and Kathy Kacer. *I Am Not a Number*. Illustrated by Gillian Newland. Toronto: Second Story Press, 2016.

* Gansworth, Eric. *If I Ever Get Out of Here*. New York: Arthur A. Levine Books/Scholastic, 2013.

* Jordan-Fenton, Christy, and Margaret Pokiak-Fenton. *Fatty Legs*. Illustrated by Liz Amini-Holmes. Toronto: Annick Press, 2010.

Loyle, Larry, with Constance Brissenden. *As Long as the Rivers Flow*. Illustrated by Heather Holmlund. Toronto: Groundwood Books, 2003.

* Santiago, Chiori. *Home to Medicine Mountain*. Illustrated by Judith Lowrey. San Francisco: Children's Book Press, 2002.

ABOUT THE AUTHOR

JOSEPH BRUCHAC is among the most respected and widely published Native American authors working today, with more than one hundred titles in print. A Rockefeller Fellow and an NEA Poetry Writing Fellow, Bruchac has received wide recognition over his long career, including the Native Writers' Circle of the Americas Lifetime Achievement Award. In addition to writing, Bruchac is an editor at Greenfield Review Press, a literary publishing house he co-founded with his wife. He lives in Greenfield Center, New York. To find out more about Joseph Bruchac, visit josephbruchac.com.

ABOUT THE ILLUSTRATOR

S. D. NELSON is the author and/or illustrator of many picture books inspired by the history and traditions of his Lakota heritage, including acclaimed biographies of Sitting Bull and Black Elk, and *Crazy Horse's Vision*, which was written by Joseph Bruchac. He is a former middle school art teacher, and his paintings are held in both private and public collections. Nelson is of Lakota (Sioux) descent and lives with his wife in Chandler, Arizona. Visit him online at sdnelson.net.